Little People, **BIG DREAMS**

MAHATMA GANDHI

Written by
Mª Isabel Sánchez Vegara

Illustrated by
Albert Arrayás

Frances Lincoln
Children's Books

This is the story of a little boy with a very big heart.
His name was Mohandas, and he lived a simple
life in a city by the Indian coast, called Porbandar.

Mohandas learned from his mother to be honest and always tell the truth. He dreamed of a world where no living thing was ever hurt, and everyone wanted the best for all.

When he was 19, Mohandas traveled to London to go to law school. At that time, the British Empire ruled his country of India. Living in London gave him the chance to learn lots of things about English culture.

With his degree in hand, Mohandas moved to South Africa to work as a lawyer. But things were not easy for Indians there.

One day, he was thrown out of a train for refusing to leave first class—a carriage that was reserved for white people only.

Mohandas decided to protest against that injustice in his very own way. He sat quietly in the middle of the street. Soon, thousands of Indians joined him. It was the first peaceful resistance movement ever.

For more than 20 years, Mohandas and his followers kept working to improve the rights of Indians in South Africa. But he wanted to go back to India and lead his country out of the bonds of the British Empire.

Back home, Mohandas took off his expensive British suit and started wearing traditional Indian clothes.

It was his way to show support to his people.

Mohandas's peaceful movement spread across India.
His supporters protested against the unfair English laws
by refusing to work and cooperate with the government.

When Britain made salt expensive to buy, Mohandas
marched 241 miles to the Indian Ocean in protest.

He harvested the salt himself to give to his people. This little gesture shook the world in the gentlest way.

Mohandas was put in jail many times for organizing these protests. Some of the people he loved most in the world died while he was imprisoned. As a way to claim his freedom, Mohandas stopped eating.

The British were scared that Mohandas might die in prison, so they decided to release him. That day, the rich and the poor celebrated together as one.

His people called him "Mahatma," meaning "great soul."

He became the father of the Indian nation and one of the most famous leaders for justice and civil rights.

And Mahatma, the little boy with the very big heart, gave a single lesson to those who hope for a brighter future: sometimes, the power of peace is greater than the power of force.

MAHATMA GANDHI

(Born 1869 • Died 1948)

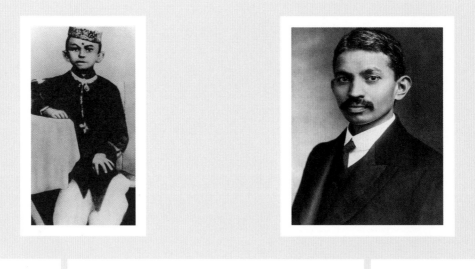

c. 1876   1921

When Mohandas was a young boy, his mother instilled core Hindu values in him that influenced his later life, like a commitment to nonviolence. He was surrounded by friends with many faiths, which also influenced his worldview. When he turned 19, Mohandas moved to England to study law. While there, he honored his cultural traditions and remained vegetarian for the duration of his stay. He qualified as a lawyer and then moved to South Africa for work. There, he was struck by the injustice Indians experienced by white settlers. Mohandas was not allowed to sit in the same train carriages as white people, and all Indian people had to have their fingerprints taken by law. This discrimination motivated Mohandas to become an activist. He organized people to defy the unfair laws peacefully—but was arrested and put in prison. Later, when he was

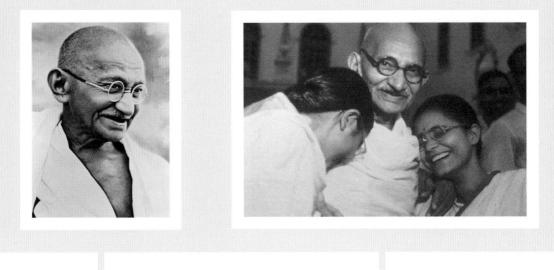

1940   1947

released, he worked to help Indian people win the right to vote in South Africa. Mohandas then turned his attention to the British Empire's rule in India. At that time, the Indian people were not allowed to vote for their own government. Mohandas led the movement to free India from the British Empire. He used nonviolent protests to resist the rule. He was arrested in 1942 for promoting the idea of independence. People were distraught and violence ran riot across the country. Gandhi was dismayed and stopped eating as a way to protest. Eventually, Britain formally left India. Some people disagreed with Gandhi for promoting peace and tolerance and tried to kill him. Sadly, one man succeeded. Today Gandhi is remembered as the "Father of India": a passionate hero who fought for freedom and opposed violence at all costs.

Want to find out more about **Mahatma Gandhi?**
Read one of these great books:

Who Was Gandhi? by Dana Meachen Rau and Jerry Hoare

I Am Gandhi by Brad Meltzer and Christopher Eliopoulos

All About Mohandas Gandhi by Todd Outcalt and Amber Calderon

BOARD BOOKS

COCO CHANEL

ISBN: 978-1-78603-245-4

MAYA ANGELOU
ISBN: 978-1-78603-249-2

FRIDA KAHLO
ISBN: 978-1-78603-247-8

AMELIA EARHART

ISBN: 978-1-78603-252-2

MARIE CURIE

ISBN: 978-1-78603-253-9

ADA LOVELACE

ISBN:978-1-78603-259-1

ROSA PARKS

ISBN: 978-1-78603-263-8

EMMELINE PANKHURST

ISBN: 978-1-78603-261-4

AUDREY HEPBURN
ISBN: 978-1-78603-255-3

ELLA FITZGERALD

ISBN:978-1-78603-257-7

BOOKS & PAPER DOLLS

EMMELINE PANKHURST

ISBN: 978-1-78603-400-7

MARIE CURIE

ISBN: 978-1-78603-401-4

BOX SETS

WOMEN IN ART

ISBN: 978-1-78603-428-1

WOMEN IN SCIENCE

ISBN: 978-1-78603-429-8

Collect the *Little People,* **BIG DREAMS** series:

FRIDA KAHLO

ISBN: 978-1-84780-783-0

COCO CHANEL

ISBN: 978-1-84780-784-7

MAYA ANGELOU

ISBN: 978-1-84780-889-9

AMELIA EARHART

ISBN: 978-1-84780-888-2

AGATHA CHRISTIE

ISBN: 978-1-84780-960-5

MARIE CURIE

ISBN: 978-1-84780-962-9

ROSA PARKS

ISBN: 978-1-78603-018-4

AUDREY HEPBURN

ISBN: 978-1-78603-053-5

EMMELINE PANKHURST

ISBN: 978-1-78603-020-7

ELLA FITZGERALD

ISBN: 978-1-78603-087-0

ADA LOVELACE

ISBN: 978-1-78603-076-4

JANE AUSTEN

ISBN: 978-1-78603-120-4

GEORGIA O'KEEFFE

ISBN: 978-1-78603-122-8

HARRIET TUBMAN

ISBN: 978-1-78603-227-0

ANNE FRANK

ISBN: 978-1-78603-229-4

MOTHER TERESA

ISBN: 978-1-78603-230-0

JOSEPHINE BAKER

ISBN: 978-1-78603-228-7

L. M. MONTGOMERY

ISBN: 978-1-78603-233-1

JANE GOODALL
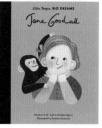
ISBN: 978-1-78603-231-7

SIMONE DE BEAUVOIR

ISBN: 978-1-78603-232-4

MUHAMMAD ALI

ISBN: 978-1-78603-331-4

STEPHEN HAWKING

ISBN: 978-1-78603-333-8

MARIA MONTESSORI

ISBN: 978-1-78603-755-8

VIVIENNE WESTWOOD

ISBN: 978-1-78603-757-2

DAVID BOWIE

ISBN: 978-1-78603-332-1

Brimming with creative inspiration, how-to projects, and useful information to enrich your everyday life, Quarto Knows is a favorite destination for those pursuing their interests and passions. Visit our site and dig deeper with our books into your area of interest: Quarto Creates, Quarto Cooks, Quarto Homes, Quarto Lives, Quarto Drives, Quarto Explores, Quarto Gifts, or Quarto Kids.

The illustrations were created with watercolor and pencil.
Set in Futura BT.

Published by Rachel Williams • Designed by Karissa Santos
Edited by Katy Flint • Production by Jenny Cundill

Manufactured in Guangdong, China CC022019

9 7 5 3 1 2 4 6 8

Photographic acknowledgments (pages 28–29, from left to right) 1. Gandhi, Mahatma, 1876 © ullstein bild, Getty 2. Early Photo of Mahama Gandhi, 1921 © Bettmann via Getty Images 3. Mahatma Gandhi, 1940 © Bettman via Getty Images 4. Mahatma Gandhi Laughing with Granddaughters, 1947 © Bettman via Getty Images